ROYAL COURT

Royal Court Theatre presents

NIGHTINGALE AND CHASE

by Zinnie Harris

First performance at the Royal Court Jerwood Theatre Upstairs,
Sloane Square, London on 28 September 2001.

Production supported by Jerwood New Playwrights.
Prison tour supported by the Jerwood Charitable Foundation.

JERWOOD
NEW PLAYWRIGHTS

Characters

Nightingale
a man in his forties

Chase
a woman in her twenties

There is something about the way that they look
that makes them an unlikely couple.

The time is the present.

NIGHTINGALE AND CHASE

One

NIGHTINGALE

I'd been working on it in my mind. I'd got it all laid
out in my mind. No problems in my mind, see? In my
mind it was straightforward. Piece of cake. Well maybe
not cake but well planned. The best I could. Thought
through. The whole evening thought through. Start
to finish.

I'd had bloody long enough to work it out, hadn't I?

But of course I go and blow it.

Mess it up.

Screw it all.

Never works the way you want, does it?

Got to be careful I said to myself. Got to be careful. Isn't
going to be easy at first. Understatement.

Isn't going to be easy for either of you. You or Chase.

And she certainly had no idea how much thinking I was
putting in. Done better than a lot of men would, didn't I?
Most men? No chance. Not all that thinking about it,
planning it. Every day. Or nearly every day. Nearly every
day for nearly a year.

Vegies, chicken, candles, fizzy wine – kid out the way.

Cleared the house. Hoovered. Chucked the rubbish out. Made the bed. Clean sheets.

Spotless.

First thing she notices the hedge.

Why do you let the hedge grow? she says.

What?

Why do you let the hedge grow? Chase again.

First thing, I can't believe it. I don't know do I? I've been busy.

Oh, she says. Lips tight. That face again. Forgotten about that face to tell you the truth.

I'll get the clippers out at the weekend if you want.

OK. Chase again.

And that is it. Practically the first thing she says. And right from then, I know it isn't going to go right, bugger the plans and all that Nightingale, nothing is going to go right. She'd been silent in the car coming home anyway. I'd been driving, of course, she sitting. Why should I be the one to make conversation? I think to myself, I am the one with my flipping eyes on the road. And she obviously didn't think it was up to her either, so we just sat there in silence the whole bloody way home. Like lemons. And that isn't a small journey. Two and a half hours we were in that car. This is up to the both of us I thought, this isn't easy for either of us. Anyway so I put a tape on, only she didn't like that. Didn't say anything of course, seeing as by then she was looking out the window and not saying anything at all. But I knew she didn't like it, well I thought if you aren't going to talk, I'm going to have the music on, that is it.

I'd thought that by the time we had got into the car we'd have got through all that to tell you the truth. In my mind we would have, see, if it had all gone the way I planned it. First thing, a kiss. Not a big slobbery one or anything, no passion but just to say hello. But she didn't want that did she, no. OK. Fair enough, OK, so no kiss, but could have been something, just a hug or something to say you are here, and I am here and it is nice to see you. But no, none of that. That was where we went wrong if you ask me. Get me home, was all she would say. Not here. Get me home. Fair enough I thought. Put her bag in the back and started driving. Tried again when we hit the motorway. Feeling OK love? I said. Got nothing back. I don't want to talk she said. Just get me home. So I put the tape on. OK, you don't want to talk, you don't have to talk. Here we go. Fleetwood Mac.

The flaming hedge. I don't know why I didn't get around to it. Is that all you can notice, says I? Why do you let it get that high? Why you so bothered about it? says I. It cuts out the light is what she tells me back. I try to shrug it off. Next weekend I say. I'll get the clippers out.

So we go in. Only she won't let me take her bag, will she? She doesn't want me to go anywhere near her. Fair enough think I. I'll leave her a minute. Cup of tea? She agrees to that though, so I think maybe we are getting somewhere. She looks around a bit. She looks around a lot. Nothing much has changed but of course she notices the small things. New clock, a hole in the wall where a shelf fell down, those sorts of things, set of old jugs that my dad gave me. She doesn't like them, straight away. She doesn't say anything of course but she doesn't need to. Cup of tea? I say. And I've got this bottle of bubbly in the fridge, but I don't think we are quite there yet so I don't mention that. It's nice to have you home, says I.

You were late she says.

Ten minutes.

Half an hour she says.

It was the traffic. You can't time these things perfectly.

I thought you weren't coming she says. Go over to her at that point, want to touch her but think I'd better not.

Of course I was coming.

Think I had better say it again, make sure she heard.

Of course I was coming.

And then she does the strangest thing. She puts her bag down and she cries. And I mean she really cries. Not her normal cry, I've heard that enough times. No, this is like a wail, sort of deep down, strangulated noise. She just stands there and makes this horrible sound. Sounds like an animal. So I go up to her, again. More gently now. Don't cry, I say, but that only makes it worse. Don't cry, please don't cry, and by now I've got my arms around her and I am almost crying myself. Don't cry Chase love, but it doesn't make any difference. She is sobbing now, really sobbing, and suddenly I am sobbing. And the pair of us are just standing there sobbing. And then she starts laughing. Just as suddenly as she started crying. I don't know if this is a joke or what. But she is holding me back now, quite tight. And that feels OK, so I start laughing. It's better to be laughing than that terrible crying. So we are holding on to each other like we never have before. And laughing.

Then I mess it up for another time. I want to kiss her again don't I? Of course I do. I always did want to jump the gun with Chase a bit. Did that even when she was younger. But she doesn't want a kiss, does she? No. She just wants to be either laughing or crying. She pushes me off. Sorry she says. No, it is me, I go. Not yet. She says. Of course go I.

And it's not time for the bubbly then either.

But I don't want her to be laughing at me. If that was what she was doing she can think again. I am not going to have her laughing at me.

Where is Scott? goes she. At my sister's go I. Well I knew she wouldn't like that, but there it is. Why isn't he here? goes she.

Course she isn't well. That is what I notice. Knew. I knew she wasn't well before, that's what got her into this mess. But she doesn't look like she is any better. And you might be thinking how the hell do I know, I'm not a bloody doctor am I? But I know all about it, from my mum being exactly the same. You give me another reason why anyone would do any of this. It's not balanced. There is food and a house isn't there? That is what my dad used to say. There is food and a house, why are you doing it? Why do we need all this other stuff? And you never get an answer. And that is why

I've got Scott round at Laura's. I need to know that she is better before this is any place for the kid.

He's at Laura's go I.

Oh. goes she. Lips tight again. Thought he might be here.

Not tonight go I.

Right. She.

Give ourselves a bit of space and time tonight. Me again.

I see. She.

And that is how we kind of leave it, about Scott anyway. I suggest she takes a bath while I put the dinner on, but she doesn't like that. She thinks I'm saying that she stinks, which I am not, although I would have thought she would have wanted a bath after spending all that time in a place like that. You don't know what it was like, she almost is yelling at me now. And I know I have to stay calm, seen it after years of watching my dad. Stay calm I says to myself, no use both of us yelling at each other. Go and have a bath I says.

But I'm not going to have her laughing at me.

She could have got the coach home anyway. She could have got the coach, and I could have picked her up at the coach station. Wouldn't have cost more than about thirteen pounds or something, we probably spent that on the petrol anyway. Might have been better, wouldn't have had to have that bloody awful silent journey anyway.

I'm not having her laughing at me, if that was what it was. I've done better than most men, and she knows it.

Next thing phone rings. Who the hell is that? Neither of us move. Eventually I answer. My boss. Hello, Nightingale goes he, that you? Course it is flaming me. What do you want, only not like that, because me and him are just settling in. Polite as ever, I am. Can I help you? go I. Wants to talk business. Not a good time I say. Try to smile at her while I am talking. Problem says he. Can't wait till tomorrow? No chance. Coming over. Not a good time I say. Too late, he's put the phone down. Problem? says she. Got a new job say I. Oh. She. The boss is coming over. Why? She again. I don't know. Me. Says something has come up. Oh, her again. You in trouble? Of course not. Oh, she again. Stop saying bloody Oh woman. I'm going for a bath, she goes. Cross now. I'll get rid of him, I say, no need for him to come in. What's he like? she goes. Bloody stupid question if you ask me, try to play dumb. My boss? Yes. I don't know. Like to meet him. No need, probably some papers or something, I'll sign them at the door. Seeing as he is coming, I would like to meet him. She again, edge in her voice now. Not tonight Chase. Know where she is going with this one, don't like it. You go and have your bath, I'll deal with the boss.

Told you see, she is not well. She has forgotten how it works in the real world, everything is so up here in her head, she doesn't remember how it all works for real.

Know about me, does he? And it is out there. I try to side-step.

What do you mean, know about you?

15

Know you have a wife? Yes says I. She isn't really my
wife, but we always said she might as well be, seeing as
we've been together since she was about sixteen and
we've had the kid and everything. I say course he does.
He doesn't actually, but that isn't what she is getting at
and me and her both know it. You see this is the thing
about her not being well, she thinks if you don't tell
every bleeding person that you have a wife in the clink it
means you are making some kind of personal attack on
her. Course I'm not going to tell my boss I've got a wife
who's been done for fraud and shop-lifting and about
every other sort of petty crime you care to mention. I'm
not that stupid. But of course she doesn't see it like that
does she?

She might when she is well again. That is all I hope.
Because she is a sensible girl, when she is herself. But in
the meantime I am not going to lose my job just because
she is not well.

Get back on the mobile when she is upstairs. Can't make
tonight mate. Oh, he. Sounding like my bleeding wife and
all. Why? Things around here are a bit iffy. Says I. Oh.
Him again. See you tomorrow though, first thing? If you
want, alright. Anything I can help with? No thank you
mate. Put the phone down as well, had enough of that
sort of help. Shout up the stairs, he isn't coming. Silence,
know what that means. Chase? You heard me love, isn't
coming. Now I've pissed off my wife and my boss.

Comes back down again. Bit later on, heard her
unpacking, not that she had much, only let you take in
about three pairs of anything those places. Had a bath
though. Looks lovely. Good enough to eat. Dinner is
nearly done, say I. Think it might be nearly time for that
bubbly, she sits down. Good bath? Say I. Alright. Lovely.

I try to talk about my new job. Big break for me. Lots of responsibility. She isn't interested. OK. I try to open the bubbly, she doesn't want that either. All this bloody food I have cooked, not wanted either. I put it in front of her, anyway. She doesn't touch it. Waste of money if you ask me, and it won't keep. God knows what she wants, she certainly isn't going to tell me.

She has this thing that I never ask her the questions, well that was exactly the same as my mother. Course I never get to ask the bleeding questions because she is always in there giving it this and that before I get the chance. And I know she wants me to ask her all about it, I can see it in her face. But I don't. I don't know why. I know enough about those places and the rest I don't need to know. I know how they work, I've asked around a bit haven't I? Know people who know more than me. What the hell does she want me to ask her anyway? Half the time she says she doesn't want to talk about it and the other half she expects you to wade in there and bring it up first.

Did they let you watch the telly?

Stupid question, I know it. She knows it. Just came out. Ten months inside and all I could think of to ask her. Flaming stupid. I told you I didn't know what to ask.

I mean I . . . I go on. I don't know what the hell I mean, and that's the truth.

She helps me out. Sometimes.

Not a stupid question after all. She can see I'm trying. She has got a gorgeous smile. Goes straight to my insides.

I'm going on again though, trying to think of the next question. Want to cash in on it, while she is still smiling.

I love you. She says.

Straight out the blue. Definitely time for the bubbly. And she comes round and gives me this bloody great kiss. Out of nowhere. Kiss her back, tell her I've missed her, because I have, I have bloody missed her. Bloody missed her like fuck. Another bloody great kiss. I have really really missed her.

And if we had got to there by the end of the evening we would have been alright. If the night could have stopped just there and we had gone to bed it would have still been like the plan. Gone upstairs, not answered the door. Had a cuddle, who knows. Sure we had gone off the path a little, but that was the aim, to get to the place where she gave me a kiss and I told her that I had missed her. That was all either of us wanted. Like that first week together, you get to a point and you know the rest of the week is going to be OK. Everything that needs to be said has been said, you can relax, you can get on with it. That is where we should have been. But she wants to talk about Scott doesn't she? That's the rub. And she knows it.

Why Laura's?

The kiss is over, I can tell that. She goes back round her side of the table.

Eat your dinner. She might as well, I spent good money on it.

Why is he at Laura's?

Because we need some space. I told you.

You don't like Laura.

Kind of true, or nearly true. She doesn't like Laura
either, in fact I would say she is the one that doesn't like
Laura, and it is me who doesn't mind her.

Laura takes good care of the kid.

I see, she goes.

How is he anyway? Her again.

Alright.

School?

OK.

Missing me?

She wants more, I can see that. I don't know what the
hell he feels about all of this, we haven't talked about it.
You'll have to ask him, I say.

Maybe I should ask Laura. Her again.

He is only there for tonight I remind her, but she doesn't
believe me, I can see she doesn't. But she is jumping the
gun now, way out of line, none of this was on the
agenda for tonight. Just like my mum when she came
out. Wanting everything all at once. What the flaming
heck was I supposed to do? She doesn't say anything, got
a glazed look. I hate that look, it says piss off you don't
know what is going on in my head. Think about that.

And think about the money I spent on the food she isn't going to eat.

She isn't going to let it go. That's for sure.

Doorbell goes. Bloody boss has come round. Answer it but only open it a crack. Just thought you might need some help. Everything OK, Nightingale? says he. Never knew he was such a bloody busybody. Like a bloody vicar coming round. Everything fine, just domestic stuff. Chase in the background shouting let him in. And he is inside and got his coat off before I can take my breath.

Chase this is the boss, boss this is Chase. Chase is an unusual name, blah blah usual stuff. Think we all need a drink. Here we go, about to lose my job. Either that or my wife. When she gets something into her head she is going to go all that way until it is done. Shut my eyes and wait for it almost. He has only given me the job because he has been ripped off in the past and he thinks he can trust me. Oh shit here we go.

Anyway we all get pissed. Turns out he turned up with a bottle of whisky. Said he bought it in case I was in the middle of a crisis, voice sounded strained on the phone. Didn't know that he took such an interest in my welfare I tell him. He doesn't laugh at that, just smiles. Decide I don't like him now, thought I was beginning to know where I stood with him, but him coming round to the house when he wasn't invited and with the wife and everything is not on. Well, he and her get on like a house on fire. Joking and laughing all over the shop. She tells him of course, turns out one of his mates is inside, no problem with that. Have a good laugh at me about that, that I thought he might mind and all, etc. etc., laugh laugh. Chase enjoying it all the while. I end up drinking more than either of them to tell the truth. Got to do something as I am the one not laughing. He smokes and she gives him the light. Laugh laugh, more drink. Oh they are enjoying themselves.

Then she goes and brings up Scott in front of him doesn't she? She is trying to use the fact that he is there to embarrass me, or something like that, I don't know what her game is any more.

Nightingale has decided I am not a fit mother to our son, she says.

Oh, goes he.

It's true isn't it? she says. He has moved him out because I have come home.

Silence.

She just stares at me.

The boss coughs, he doesn't know what to think.

My wife isn't well I tell him.

THERE IS NOTHING BLOODY WRONG WITH ME NIGHTINGALE AND YOU KNOW IT she goes.

Silence again.

It is his mum that was the flaming psycho.

There was no need for that I tell her.

There was every bloody need for it she tells me back.

Boss stands up. I should be going he says.

You don't have to she goes. Stay, have another drink she goes.

Silence.

No I should be going he says, and puts on his coat.

And out he goes. Pretty sharpish. Way too pissed to be driving but that is his lookout. Why should I say anything?

Shut the door. Alone again.

Fucking bloody evening. Feeling pretty annoyed now, can feel it throbbing through my arms and legs. Think about going out for a walk, calm down, seen my dad do that enough times, then think no. She asked for this, might as well let her have it. You want the truth I say Chase, the truth, here is the truth.

You are right. Scott doesn't live here any more.

But I didn't move him out just for the night. He hasn't lived here all the time you have been away.

He lives with Laura.

She knew it anyway. Can see that. What the fuck was I supposed to do I want to scream at her. You weren't here, I'd just got a new job, I didn't want having the kid to go and screw it up. I still see him Tuesdays don't I? And at the weekends. I am doing my bloody best Chase, and you know it.

When is he moving back in? Her. Here we go, me. In my head though, I think that, don't say it. He isn't. Why not? You know how it goes, I say a line she says a question. He isn't moving in Chase because you aren't well, and I am not having him here with you until you are better. Well she goes off the handle at that. Throws a glass at me, chucks the rest of the booze in my face, starts to hit me. Oh no this wasn't how it was supposed to go at all. You need to get better, that is all I keep telling her. She has this thing of course that she isn't ill. And then of course she starts screaming about my mum. I'm not her she goes over and over, I am not her. Scott isn't you, if anyone is ill, it is you, not me.

And that is when I screw it up for both of us. She won't stop yelling. I hear her screaming, and in my head I am just watching her calm, like my dad. But it isn't what my arms are doing, they are doing this other thing. This hard thing, that screws it up.

Next thing she is on the floor.

And then she is out of here.

I hold the door open for her. But I don't follow her out. Close the door, she has gone. Fuck to myself.

I scrape the food into the bin. I mop the booze up off the floor. I run my hand under the cold tap. I lock up. I go to bed.

Fuck.

Blackout.

Two

CHASE

I am not coming back Nightingale.

I am not coming back.

I am never fucking well coming back.

Fucking tosser.

Walk down the street still saying that over and over. Bloody head hurts like fuck. And it is flipping cold out here. Like the bloody North Pole all of a sudden. Don't know why they go on about global warming all the time. It's freezing. Bit of blood down the back of my neck, only part of me that feels warm. Don't know where the fuck I am going, but I am not going back there. See a phone box, go inside. Not exactly the Ritz but just need a place out of the wind, to get myself sorted. Bloody stinks of bloody piss and vomit mind.

I am not going back there. Ever.

Pick the phone up without thinking.

Get a 20 p out. Hear the beeps. Listen for a minute.

Need someone to come and get me. Take me somewhere else or something. Now. Get me out of here.

Start dialling.

Think about phoning my dad.

Keep forgetting he is supposed to be dead.

According to my mum he is anyway. And my mum is abroad.

Think about phoning Buzz or Anne or one of that lot.

They wouldn't give a toss. You got a phone box to sleep in? You're alright then.

Think about phoning Laura. Or Scott. Could ask to speak to Scott.

Bloody great idea. Hello Scott, it's your mum here, I'm bleeding my head away because your dad just tried to brain me in the kitchen.

Think about phoning him back at the house.

Put the phone down. Can't do that. Stupid voice on the other end had come on and had started telling me to put it down anyway. Thank you missus, nick of time. Always do what I am told anyway. 20 p comes out the bottom. I'll have that back and all.

Fuck. Hit the phone, that hurts my finger a bit but I don't care. Hit it again. No one I know is going to come out this time of night to come and pick me up, are they? Got fuck all people to phone. No one I know would give a shit. Only him, and I am not going back there. Going to have a fucking great bruise on the back of my head, I can feel it. Come out of the phone box, keep walking although it has started raining and at least in the phone box I wasn't getting wet. Find a pub, that is all I need to do. One of the all-night bars, or a club, somewhere to sit until morning is all I need. Still wearing my tracksuit and my trainers, but anything goes in clubs these days doesn't it? I don't know. When was the last time I went to a flipping club? I'm going to have to work it out in the morning, need to find somewhere to go and think, that is all. Somewhere you can go in a tracksuit. Wish I'd eaten all that bloody food now. Fucking chicken and roast potatoes. Making my mouth water thinking of all that food I didn't go anywhere near. Bet he has eaten it by now. Bet he has eaten the whole bloody thing by now. Been starving since this morning.

Feel sick.

Actually.

Feel very sick.

Think I might throw up. Stand and get my breath again.

Phew.

Gone. Haven't felt sick like that since I was pregnant with Scott. Can't be bloody pregnant that is one thing I know.

Turn into the next street. Slowly, head still swimming. All the windows dark. Everyone in the fucking street gone to bed already. God knows what the time is. And it's cold. Head is hurting, again. Stopped bleeding now, but only just. That would have been great, come out of prison only to be killed on my first night home. Got to keep thinking, got to keep thinking about where the bloody hell I can go. Think think think, where the fuck can you go? Not going back to the house. Getting

fucking noisy up there in my head now. All these things
I have got to be thinking about.

See a police car at the end of the road, sitting outside the
chippy. Just sent someone in for some chips, either that
or they are doing a bust. Could go and tell them they've
got someone who bloody nearly murdered me down at
Number 40. Fuck that, won't listen anyway. Walk past.
They look at me though. What you doing out at this
time of night? Thinking, can see it in their faces. Bloody
faces up their arse. Running away that is what. Yes,
tracksuit and all. Running away. Why the hell else do
you think I am called Chase?

Seem to keep walking anyway, with fuck idea of where
I am going. Police car way behind me now. Haven't
moved. Still sitting, eating their chips. They weren't
bothered. Lone woman out in the middle of the night,
why the hell should they give a fuck? Blood down the
back of her head. So what? They are only suppose to be
protecting people like me. I've nearly been half-murdered
mate. Tomorrow going to get a place. Go to the social,
get it sorted. Got to get Scott back. Not having bloody
Scott with bloody Laura.

Seem to end up at the bus station. At least it is open.
They don't mind if you sit there for an hour or two.
Been here plenty times before. Look at the bus timetables
to make it look like I know where I am going. Got
twenty-four pounds in my pocket in case anyone asks.
Leeds or Liverpool. Seem to be stuck by the L's. Trying
to take a step along the timetable but I'm still by the L's.
Not going back up bloody north, just spent my time up
there. Just spent the last day on the motorway. Why
would I want to go back up there? Leicester. Luton.
Lymehouse. Eventually find the M's. Manchester. Knew a

27

girl in Manchester once, Maidenhead, that is too bloody near here. Morecambe. Morecambe Bay. Never been to Morecambe. Sit back down again. Bet it costs more than twenty-four pound though, and then there is Scott. If I piss off to Morecambe never going to get him back, am I?

Should have got a bus home anyway. Shouldn't have fucking asked him to come and pick me up in the first place. Oh he bloody loved it, him having to do something for me. Me having to ask him. Like it has always been.

He thinks I have ruined my life. I know he does. He certainly thinks I have ruined his.

Played this game. Inside, with the other girls. The 'he is going to meet you' game. The 'he is going to meet you with flowers' game. The 'he is going to turn up in a limo' game. The 'he is going to bring champagne' game. The 'he is going to cover you in kisses, or love-bites, or cum, or bloody Belgian chocolate, doesn't matter but when you walk out of those gates, he is going to be there', that is the game. And of course they never are. That is also the game. And you know all your mates are watching you out the window, those that can see you leave, and you know they are waiting to see who turns up for you. Ten months no limos. One girl was met with flowers. One girl. Often they don't even come at all. Send someone else, or you just have to walk by yourself to the bus.

Mine. Nearly three-quarters of an hour late. Arrives with nothing. Clapped out old banger and bad breath. Tries to shag me before we even get home and the night ends with him trying to punch my lights out. That would have given the other girls a laugh anyway. Oh yes, the other girls they would have loved that.

Sandra. That's the name of the girl in Manchester.

Look up the price of a ticket to Manchester. Fifty-five pound. Bloody fifty-five pound, who do they think they are? It's only a flaming bus. And then there is Scott. Can't keep forgetting about him. If I go to Manchester, that is it. He will be stuck at Laura's for ever. I will never get him back.

No one else much in the bus station. See a bus come in, everyone gets off it. Look tired. Reckon it has been delayed. Someone comes up to me asks the time. I don't flaming know haven't had a watch for about four years. Sorry missus I didn't mean to say that. Other people look at me, think I am sleeping rough. Got twenty-four pounds in my pocket, could go to a bed and breakfast if I wanted. Got a home, could go home if I wanted. Or to Laura's, she has got nice beds. Nice house. Lots of nice food, and she has got lots of nice things. She has got my flaming nice son.

Don't need to sleep anyway. Done so much bloody sleeping in the last ten months, all you ever do is sleep when you are in there. Slept so much won't care if I never sleep again. Eat though I do need to do. Reckon I am going to end up spending the whole twenty-four pound on breakfast if I am not careful.

Another bus comes in. Think I recognise someone but I don't. Nearly call out to them, then change my mind last minute. Turn it into a cough. Don't think she notices.

Where the fucking hell am I going to go?

Promised myself two things. Ten months, had quite a time to do the promising. Three things. Sorry, three things not two. One: I am not going to let anyone tell me I am depressed. Two: I am not doing the cheque books or the lifting any more. Three: I am going to be a good mother to Scott.

Tomorrow, get a place in a hostel. Know a woman who went there, she said it was alright. Sometimes they help you get a job, get back on your feet. Married too young probably. Everyone said I did. Had Scot too young anyway. Or at least I was too young, he was bloody ancient before we even started.

He grew that hedge so no one could see me. I know that. And he knows I know that. He doesn't want anyone to see me. Find out where I've been. Keep me covered by a flaming bit of greenery. It was alright when I was inside probably. Told them all I left him most likely. Would have loved that. Chase? Oh Chase – she left, mate. She's upped and gone. Poor old Nightingale they would say. Serves him right for marrying someone so young.

Fucking freezing. Was looking forward to a night under a duvet again and all. Shitty little blankets they give you inside. And if you ask for another one, that is it. Oh no they don't like that, you can't complain about anything in there.

Decide I had better walk again. Can't sit still. Going to turn into a statue if I stay there all night. Everyone wake up in the morning see this new statue there, where the fucking hell that come from, they would say. Looks fantastic. Looks just like a woman. Just like a woman who is starving and freezing and has got a bloody great bruise on the back of her head. But a woman all the same. And there I would be, dead and covered in pigeon shit for the rest of time. And people would stub out their cigarettes against my face. Not worth it, better move.

He is probably out looking for me by now anyway. Reckon he will come here in the end and don't want him to find me.

Turn up at the hostel just as they are all having breakfast. Remembered the address from that woman who went there. Can't remember her name, but remember the street. The place smells fantastic. Give them bacon and eggs if they ask for it. Nearly go and swipe this plate off this old woman as she is sitting there. Think I had better not, not if I want them to give me a place, don't want them to think I am any trouble. I'm not anyway. They have got a room, but they need to phone my probation blah blah. Go ahead. Standing in the office, don't like the way the woman is looking at me, but want the place so don't say anything. Pulled my hood up so she can't see the blood. She says I am lucky. Don't feel lucky, ask her why. Someone died, they've got a room free. Not so lucky for the swine who died, says I. No indeed goes she. Not a joker, I can say that for her. Am going to see I am going to have to watch that one. No sign of a sense of humour there that is for sure.

Takes me up to the room. So small you can't open the door past the wardrobe. Better not put any weight on while I am here or else I'll never be able to get out again. Think of making another joke of it, but think I had better not. Not with a face like hers. She wants to know where my stuff is. I tell her about last night. She doesn't care I can see that. She has heard it all before. So another bloke hit someone so big deal. Just like the woman dying in the night. No big deal to anyone around here. Nothing is a big deal.

Bloody great long list of rules though. That is a big deal. It's easy as long as you don't try and do anything. Sit in your room all day and don't do anything and you should be OK. Sit there and get high thinking about tomorrow's breakfast.

The woman who had the big plate of bacon comes round later. You new she says? She's got no teeth I can say that for her. What happened to the woman who was in this room? I ask her. What woman? The woman who died? No one died. She said. The woman who was in this room died, last night, I says. Who told you that? The woman downstairs. What woman? goes she. Flipping mental this place, if you aren't half balmy before you come in you sure are going to be by the time you come out. The woman who let me in, gave me the room. I don't know, she says. I don't know about anyone dying. And she goes off. They never tell us anything in here, she goes. Takes her flipping gums with her. Who knows whether anyone did die or not, but one thing is for sure, this place gives me the creeps.

Next woman I meet is called Hester. Great big woman. Good name for a guinea pig I say. She doesn't get it. Neither do I. Don't know why I flipping said it. She asks me what happened to my head, I tell her I fell down some stairs. She laughs. I tell her I had a fight with a train. She laughs again. I tell her I got hit by a flying guinea pig. I tell her I've got a geriatric husband who can't keep his temper. She stops laughing. I laugh my head off at that. She thinks I should go and see a doctor, but it isn't even bleeding now and I hate doctors.

One thing I will say for Hester though is she is clever. She might be scary but she doesn't take any shit. Not like I do. She takes me round the house, showing me whose is what and what is where. Everyone says hello

Hester like they are frightened not to. She goes hello back like she is the boss. Not those women downstairs. Suppose it is reasonable with tits that size. She could squash you flat as good as look at her. Could hide a person between her cleavage and no one would know the difference. See that I had better keep on her good side and all. The kitchen and living room is in one. Get a tiny little shelf in there to myself. To keep your food on, she says. Have to cook for yourself in here. And my chair. Every one has a chair, in front of the telly. When you have cooked your dinner you are supposed to sit in your chair. Can't sit in anyone else's, mind. Get into bloody great trouble for that. My chair hasn't got any seat left hardly. Great bloody bit of wood hanging down. Worst chair in the room. Don't worry she said, there is a Burger King across the road. She lights up a fag. She gives it to me and gets another one for herself. How are you going to get your stuff she says? What stuff? You can't live in that tracksuit can you? I look down, see that blood is all down the front. Hadn't noticed that. I take the cig. I'm not worried about my bleeding stuff, I say. I am worried about my bleeding son. How are you going to get your son? she says.

Then I make a fool of myself again. Starts with my eyes going wet then bloody starts coming down my cheek. Can't believe in that room with about blinking twenty-five people watching, all sitting on their chairs and telly blaring and none of them know who the hell I am, and there I am blubbing my eyes out. Never met a single one of them in my life before and I have to go and do that in front of them. I managed to survive ten months inside without a single tear, and wham twenty-four hours out and I am blubbing all over the shop. Next thing the fag is taken off me and I am being squashed to the great bosom of Hester, hard, get the bloody hairy wool of her

33

jumper up my nose. Makes me want to sneeze and I can hardly breathe. And can smell her sweat. Smells like bread that has gone off. Mouldy. Underarm smell. She tells everyone else to piss off and they have gone, just like that, all out of their chairs and back to their rooms. Running. I told you they were scared of her. I'm still crying though aren't I? I don't know what the fuck I am crying about I try to say, I think it is the lack of food or my head or something. She doesn't mind, there there she goes, my head still under her arms as if I was a baby. Her baby.

I'll help you get your son she says. I don't know how the bloody hell, I say. We'll think of something she says. Know where he is? Sort of, I say. I know the school. Can't bring him here though can I? That is another one of those rules. NO CHILDREN.

She takes me back to her room. She is pretending she is my mum now or something I think. I don't mind, I need a mum. Even if she smells of mushroom. She lends me a jumper though, bloody great thing, empty bags where the tits should be, comes down to my knees. She laughs when she sees that, but better than going with blood down my shirt. I'd get arrested probably. Hanging around a school and looking like a nutter. I wash my hair too in her sink. Feel the cut, not as bad as I thought it might be, bloody hurts though when the water gets into it. She lends me her shampoo, that smells like moudly bread and all. She is alright though, Hester. Better than bloody nobody. Better than sitting in the bus station by myself again. Feel like phoning home. Don't know why, just wonder what is going on, what he is doing. Think of him in the living room, getting ready for work. Have another little cry, don't know what has got into me lately all this bloody crying. She doesn't see that one luckily so I don't get squashed up against her again.

34

The thing is I have been with him all my life practically. Since I can remember. I don't know any different. And him and me and Scott were a family.

Get on to the bus. Know where I am going sort of. Hester doesn't like buses. Can see why – she hardly fits into them seats. Don't say anything but can see that she is having difficulty. Has to sit sideways with her legs squashed up. I sit behind her, don't say anything. Not getting squashed into those bloody tits again, not for anything.

Get to the school just as break is finishing. See the last of the kids going back in. She lights up another fag. Gives me one. Lights the second one for her. See she is OK Hester, she will always give you the first one that she lights, and have the second for her. She is a good like that. Anyway we wait until the schools lunch break, just sitting there on the wall. Couple of people walk past and look at us a bit. Couldn't care less really. Hester booms hello, at them just like she was still in the hostel. And playing at being boss. They don't say anything back of course, just look at us thinking bloody nutters. I get really nervous sitting there. Don't say anything, but neither does she thank God so it is almost like I am by myself for a second. God knows what he told Scott about me. Could have been anything. Certainly never even brought him in to see me I know that. Said it wasn't the sort of place a kid should be taken. Well that is shit because the visitors' places are OK, and they have toys and that, even if Scott is too old for toys. It is all because of him when he was a kid, I know that. Him and his mum and the way that he was made to visit her inside every week for four years.

Mind you she was crazy so fuck knows what that was like.

Lunch bell goes. Really nervous by now. Feeling a bit light-headed after all the cigarettes we have just smoked. Hester just lights one from the next, even if you haven't finished the first yet. Here you are she goes, every bloody two seconds. Have to smoke my hardest to keep up with the woman. In that hour we sat there waiting we smoked our way through the best part of three packets. That is sixty-odd cigs. Whole pile of fag butts growing at our feet.

Scott sees me from the door. I can see he does. He starts running up, then stops. Then just walks slowly like he is thinking. Poor kid doesn't know what to do. Come back, go in. All fucking to do with what Laura has told him. He does come up though, in the end. Doesn't say anything, just looks at us through the railings.

I just look back. Can't think of anything to say either.

Just stay there, both of us. Just looking.

Hester coughs. Very nearly chokes herself on her fag.

Then she laughs. Silly cow.

Have you come back now, Mum?

Fucking hell, start to feel weird again. Head pounds. Tell him to come around this other side of the railings. I want to talk to him.

Shakes his head. Isn't allowed.

Who says?

Teachers.

Which teachers?

Say we aren't allowed out of the playground.

Just be a minute love. Won't take a minute.

He shakes his head again. He's not coming.

I'll have a word with your teachers?

Have you come back now, Mum?

Have to get a breath. Can't let him see that I am upset.

Yes. Yes I've come back now.

Am I going to live with you again?

I bloody hope so darling.

All these other kids around by now. Come to have a look, see what is going on. Bloody nosey parkers.

Is this your mum? They go. He doesn't say anything to that.

Got to go, he says to me.

Alright.

And he is going. Being pulled away by the other kids.

I shout, I'll be here. When you come out later, I'll be here, alright Scott?

I love you, Mum. Mouthed as he looks over his shoulder. Or something. Think it was that. I love you too, baby.

And he is off. Gone. Back with the other kids. Somewhere round the other side of the playground with them. Gone.

Hester hands us another bloody fag. Don't want it. Stand up instead.

Right, an hour and a half. Twenty-four pound in my pocket. Come on Hester, stop all that bloody smoking woman. Clean up your act a bit. When he comes out at home time I am going to show him that I love him. The best. Better than Laura, and Nightingale and all that crap. I am his mum and I love him the best. Got about an hour and a half. Not the first clue what he is into these days but twenty-four pounds to do it. There is a shopping arcade at the end of the road. You coming or not?

Blackout.

Three

NIGHTINGALE

Next day. Afternoon. I'm at work. Phone goes. Mr
Nightingale? Yes? It's the school. A Mrs Someone. Hello
there. It's Scott, she goes. Yes. What about Scott? Been
in a fight, she goes. No I go, can't be. Not Scott. Yes she
goes. Scott. Came back in after lunch and broke some
kid's nose. Fucking hell. Why, I go? No one knows, she
answers. We thought you might know. Don't ask me,
I tell her. I'm only his father. Then she goes on a bit,
woman is in shock you can hear that. Blood all over the
other kid. Yes yes. Yes I'll come down. Yes yes, of course
I will. Well that is what she wanted in the first place
anyway, me to come down and do her job for her.

Put the phone down. Pick it up again. Ring Laura. Why
do you give them my bloody work number? You are
supposed to be looking after him. I think it's Chase she
says. I think she's been down there. I put the phone
down. All I need.

Go and see the boss. Need an afternoon off I tell him.
Everything alright? Doing the bloody vicar bit again.
Everything fine I say, except I have son who is a
delinquent and a wife who I haven't seen since the middle
of the night. Get in the car, go down to the school.
Takes me ages to find the right bloody classroom, and
everywhere I go they are playing the fucking recorder.
When I get there Scott is in tears. So is this other kid,
although Scott gave him a bloody great smacker I can
see that. What do you do that for? I say. No answer.
You said sorry yet? Nothing. Just the same as his mother.

Nothing. You are in trouble, do you know that? He nods.
Big trouble. He knows that alright.

Take him by the hand. Apologise again to the teacher.
I'll give him a talking-to when I get home I say to her.
Apologise to the other kid's mum and all. She isn't happy
I can tell that. We will get to the bottom of it, don't worry,
I say again to the teacher. Which means that Laura will,
this is her bloody department not mine. Getting anything
out of Scott is like drawing blood from a stone. He can
keep his mouth well and truly shut when he wants to.

Try to get him back to the bloody car as fast as I can,
getting fed up of all these bloody stupid women looking
at me like I don't know how to control my own son.
All looking down their noses at the pair of us. Only
he won't bloody walk to the car will he. Digs his heels
in and won't go anywhere. Starts crying again. Am
going to have to bloody carry him at this rate. Says he
wants to finish the day. Says he doesn't want to go
home yet. Can't get it out of him why, wants to sit in
the playground and wait until going home time. It's OK,
I tell him, the teachers said you could come home early.
I don't want to go. Him again.

Laura is right. Chase has been here. There is only one
person that has this effect on Scott and that is his
mother. We are going home and that is the end of it I tell
him. If you aren't going to walk then I will have to drag
you by your hair and if your hair falls out I will drag
you by your scalp but one way or the other I will get
you into that car.

He moves it after that. Very sharpish. Oh he can move
quite quickly when he wants to.

Take him round to Laura's. Clean him up a bit. Still got all this other kid's blood on him. Flipping hope this other kid hasn't got anything I think to myself. Even primary teachers are supposed to wear gloves these days aren't they?

She knows how to be with him. She is brilliant, Laura, puts him in a bath first then feeds him spaghetti hoops. I tell her that he is still in trouble she mustn't forget that he hit some guy, but she say that can come later. At least he has stopped bloody crying.

That is all I care about.

What are you going to do about Chase?

So I tell Laura everything. She knows most of it anyway. You had better go and see her she says. I don't know where she is. Ring the probation, she goes. Someone must know, she can't have just bloody disappeared. She'll be at the school I say. So go to the school.

Well I put it off a bit. Haven't exactly told Laura everything. Not everything everything. Thought she didn't need to know the whole thing anyway. She can't understand why I haven't gone already. In the end I go just to shut her up, all the aggro is making the kid cry again, and that is just about doing my head in.

Drive around for a bit, don't go straight there. Need a second or two to think how to play this one.

Chase is there already of course, sitting on the wall outside the gates. Bloody great pile of bags with her. And this other woman. Bloody weird-looking woman I can tell you that. Looks German or something to me, ugly as sin anyway. Makes our Chase look like Marilyn Monroe. I want to talk to her by herself, but she says she isn't going anywhere without this Hester or whatever her name is. She is furious I can see that, wants to see Scott and wants to see him now. I tell her she can see him, but not at the moment, I have taken him back to Laura's. She is just about to go crazy by this point. She starts trying to hit me, and kick me. Bite me, any way she can to get her nails in. I hold her off of course, she fucking hurts me but I am careful I don't lay a finger on her back. More careful than I was yesterday.

We need to talk. All I keep saying. We need to talk.

Eventually she calms down again. She is in tears again. She looks a state actually I can see that. She has got a bruise on the side of her head that I am not proud of. Want to put my arms around her, tell her it is OK, but think I had better not, because apart from anything this other woman is there and she looks bloody terrifying. Wouldn't like to get into a tangle with her and it looks like if I put a step out of place she is going to thump me one. So I say I will give her a lift. Them a lift. I will take them to wherever they want to go, somewhere where we can talk. I'm not coming back to the house, she says. OK. Laura's she says. We can't go there. Why not? You know why not. It isn't fair on Laura.

She has got all these bags with her. Shopping bags. Don't know what is in them but I know she didn't have much money when she came out. Think I had better not ask. Put them in the car. Don't say a word.

They are for Scott, she says when she sees me looking at them.

OK, I say. Nothing more.

I had twenty-four pounds on me.

Fine.

We get in the car. Bit of a squish for big tits there, but that isn't my problem. Start driving.

Eventually we end up back at her hostel. Bloody miserable place. Just opposite the Burger King. Been to the Burger King many times but never knew there was a hostel opposite. She would be much better off back with me I tell her. She doesn't say anything to that, we go inside. Men aren't allowed in this place, but they sneak me upstairs. We sit in Chase's room, hardly get the three of us in and what with that weirdo hanging around like a bad smell. Taking up all the room. Can't she buzz off? I ask her. No, says Chase, she is my chaperone. Why do you need a chaperone, I'm your husband aren't I? In case, she says. In case what? In case you decide to go on a thumping spree again. Bloody weird-looking chaperone I can tell you. If it wasn't for those enormous knockers I would say that that chaperone was a man herself.

Anyway we are just sitting there not really getting anywhere. She says she doesn't care where she lives or what happens to her but she can't be without Scott. That is fair enough say I, but we have got to come at these things slowly. No one wants you to be without Scott I tell her. You said last night she says. That was for now, I said. I don't know what I was saying.

Feel like we are getting somewhere.

At least she has calmed down.

She tells the greebo to go. Are you sure says the ape man? Yes goes Chase. Thank the Lord for that, take

43

your bloody smelly armpits with you. She didn't like me saying that, thought she was going to come back in and do for me, but I can see that Chase is hiding a smile. Of course we are going to have Scott back with us, I tell her.

Then we talk about my mum.

I didn't like it at first. Never like it when she brings her up. Laura doesn't like it either, neither of us like her to be mentioned at all if we can help it. Chase has this thing that I treat her like my mum, who was a depressive or whatever you call it and not at all well. I don't think I do, but Chase sees it differently. And she says Laura is worse. All I know is that I don't want us to argue again. I'll try not to I say. She says she isn't my mum and Scott isn't me, and that the sooner I learn that the better we will all become.

I put my arm out to her. She takes it, which feels sort of nice. Me and her belong together and she knows it.

I say I am sorry about last night.

I ask her where she went.

The bus station she goes, then here.

You sat in the bus station, by yourself?

Didn't have anywhere else to go she says.

Does your bruise hurt I ask?

A little goes she.

Have you eaten anything yet I say?

44

No she says. She has smoked that much she forgot all about food.

Are you hungry I say?

Yes. Goes she.

How about you and me go and get Scott from Laura's and the three of us go for a Chinese? I say.

She smiles again. That magic smile. Me and you and Scott are going to be OK, I say.

Door flings open. Brilliant timing. Uh oh think I, the chaperone back to make sure that nothing is going on. But no it is these other women. Chase seems to know one of them. Looks official, wears a tweed suit. Anyway they are up and hauling me out of there before I can get my breath. Then I realise that it is Chase they are after not me, they manhandle her up and down the stairs before I realise what is going on.

Hey you, don't touch her like that?

Two policeman standing downstairs.

Oh shit goes I, to myself. The bags. Still in the car.

They take Chase into this room, she is screaming now, trying to get out of their grip. Hey, I try to say I am coming in, that they can't take her anywhere without me being there, but all I get is the door slammed in my face.

My name is Andrew Nightingale I shout, and she is my wife.

I try and open it, the policeman is standing on the other side. Hey you I shout, that is my wife in there. Next thing they are taking her out of there and into the car outside. I manage to touch her hair as she passes. She has got a bruise be careful of her, I shout.

The other policeman stops me, female one. Wait a minute sir. We want to have a look in your car sir. Why? I ask. She's been seen on a store camera, she goes. They have a suspicion that they will find stolen goods. She is on licence I say. We know, she goes.

It doesn't look good, does it? she goes. Silly bitch.

Open your boot, sir, she goes.

Fuck. See Chase watching me from the police car. What can I do? Can't exactly not open the car for the policeman can I? End up being taken down the station myself.

Open the boot, sir, she goes.

So I open it. Look inside. Bags and bags full of stuff. Trainers, computer games. Soft toys. You name it she got it for the kid. She was right – Scott would have loved all this stuff.

I'm sorry, I mouth at Chase.

They were for Scott she mouths back.

Stolen? The policeman asks me. I don't know do I? I say. If Chase says not, then not. Come on says the woman, you think we were born yesterday? They were for our son, I say. Oh yeah? goes the woman. Yeah I go. She was trying to be a good mum.

The policewoman writes it all down anyway. The bags are taken out of my boot. What about Chase I ask?

Policewoman shakes her head, well that is back with the courts now isn't it? She shuts the boot. I will let you get away she says, walking towards the other police car.

I'm not going anywhere without Chase I go.

Suit yourself, says the policewoman and they drive off. Chase inside. Put the flashing lights on. No fucking need for it, but they are like that the police.

She was trying to be a good mum, I say again, but everyone has gone.

Gone.

Didn't even get a chance to wave.

Get in the car. Turn it on. Take the fucking Fleetwood Mac tape out and throw it out the window.

Drive home.

Ring Laura. Scott OK there for the night is he? Asleep she says. Alright, go I.

Put the phone down.

Go into the fridge. Nothing. Open a can of lager.

Nothing.

Think about Chase.

Nothing.

Fuck.

   Blackout.

47